IMAGES
of America

Route 66 in Texas

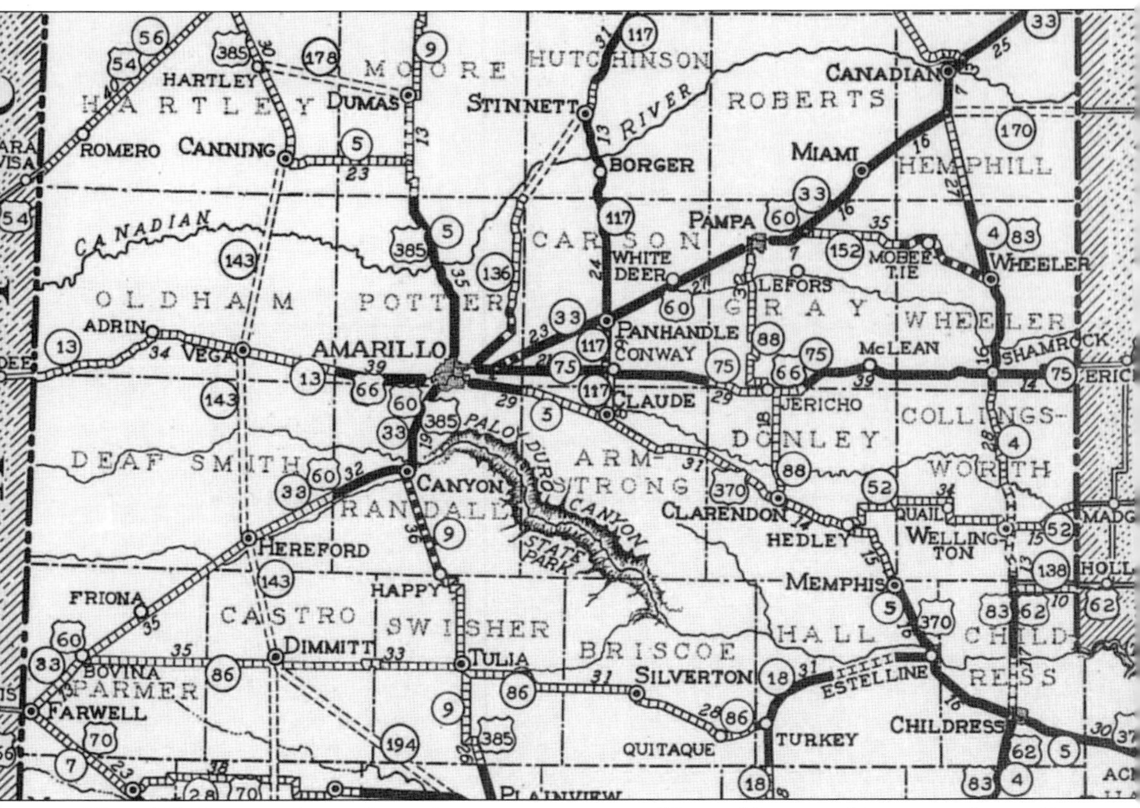

This 1933 Texas road map shows that a major portion of Route 66 was nothing more than a dirt road at that time. The dirt segments included the infamous Jericho Gap in Donley County and the section west of Bushland to Glenrio. Route 66 was also still marked State Highways 75 and 13.

On the Cover: This Magnolia station was one of the first encountered by westbound Route 66 travelers after entering Texas. The Texas Highway Department operated one of its information and welcome centers next door beginning in 1938. Magnolia was a subsidiary of Mobil. A restored Magnolia station can be seen in Shamrock a couple of blocks off Route 66.

IMAGES
of America

ROUTE 66 IN TEXAS

Joe Sonderman

ISBN 978-1-4671-3004-2

Published by Arcadia Publishing
Charleston, South Carolina

Printed in the United States of America

Library of Congress Control Number: 2013938345

For all general information, please contact Arcadia Publishing:
Telephone 843-853-2070
Fax 843-853-0044
E-mail sales@arcadiapublishing.com
For customer service and orders:
Toll-Free 1-888-313-2665

Visit us on the Internet at www.arcadiapublishing.com

For all the destinations you've brought me to,
For the people you've brought into my life,
For the history I have learned along the way,
And especially for teaching me to slow down and enjoy the journey,
Old Route 66, I will always love you.

In memory of Bob Waldmire.

Contents

Acknowledgments

Thanks to the fellow Route 66 collectors, Steve Rider and Mike Ward, who always come through for me. This book would not have been possible without the research done by Jim Ross and Jerry McLanahan. Thanks also to David Wickline, Nick Gerlich, Mark Potter, Russell Olsen, and Rich Dinkela II. Special thanks to Anne Cook at the Texas Department of Transportation and Delbert Trew at the Devil's Rope and Old Route 66 Museum in McLean. Thanks to Jim Hinckley for your inspiration and support. Unless otherwise noted, all images are courtesy of the author.

Introduction

Route 66 stretches 178 miles across the Texas Panhandle, through seven counties. To the traveler on Interstate 40, it may seem like an endless expanse with the horizon outside the towns interrupted only by the occasional grain elevator. But there is history, scenery, and adventure waiting on Route 66.

When Francisco Vasquez de Coronado crossed this area searching for the fabled cities of gold, he described it as "level as the sea." The Spanish called the vast land Llano Estacado, meaning "stockaded plain," for the fortress-like shape of its escarpments. Capt. R.B. Marcy was blazing a trail from Forth Smith, Arkansas, to Santa Fe in 1849 when he described it as "a vast illimitable expanse of desert prairie . . . which has been and must continue to be uninhabited forever."

The establishment of the J.A. Ranch by Charles Goodnight and John Adair in 1876 marked the beginning of permanent settlement, and the arrival of the railroads opened up vast areas of cheap farm and grazing land.

Roads were accorded little interest as long as the cattle could get to the railhead. A good roads association was formed in 1903, and in 1906, residents petitioned for a road between Amarillo and Claude. Demand for good roads grew as the number of autos increased, but Texas was one of the last states to provide aid for roads.

Across the nation, private promoters began laying out their own highways, giving them fancy names and colorful symbols. Most made money from towns and merchants that paid to be on the route and motorists were often routed miles out of their way. By 1924, there were over 250 such trails in the United States, promoted by over 100 different groups. The route that became US 66 was known as the Postal Highway east of Amarillo and the Ozark Trail west of Amarillo.

The Ozark Trails Association was founded by William H. "Coin" Harvey to promote a network of roads serving his Monte Ne Resort in Arkansas. The main route came into Amarillo from Wellington and then headed west, connecting with the National Old Trails Road at Las Vegas, New Mexico. The 1919 book *Ozark Trails Route* made no special mention of Amarillo. Vega and Glenrio were the only Texas communities highlighted as "live towns that are taking a public spirited interest in promoting this route." In other words, they paid.

The Texas Highway Department was formed in 1917 and began marking state routes in the 1920s. Route 66 would be cobbled together from portions of State Routes 75, 5, and 13.

In 1925, the federal government appointed a board to lay out a national highway system. Cyrus Avery of Oklahoma, the "Father of Route 66," was a member; he made sure the important highway from Chicago to Los Angeles would pass through his hometown of Tulsa.

The board mapped out a grid with the main north-south routes ending in the numbers one or five. The most important east-west routes were assigned a number ending in zero and Avery's Chicago-to-Los Angeles route was given the number 60. But Gov. William J. Fields of Kentucky demanded the important-sounding 60 for the route through his state. Angry telegrams flew until Avery and his supporters agreed to accept the catchy sounding "66."

The new federal routes went into effect on November 11, 1926. But Route 66 was a great highway in name only. In Texas, not a single mile of concrete had been poured, and motorists had to open gates between Shamrock and Amarillo. The first hard-surfaced section was in San Jacinto Heights, paved with brick in 1927.

Avery spearheaded the formation of the US 66 Highway Association to promote the highway as "The Main Street of America." The association saw a transcontinental footrace over Route 66 from Los Angeles to Chicago and then on to New York City as a golden opportunity. Sports promoter and showman C.C. "Cash and Carry" Pyle offered a $25,000 first prize. He planned to charge communities to host the race and the accompanying sideshow attractions.

On March 4, 1928, a racially diverse group of 199 runners began the grueling journey from the Ascot Raceway in Los Angeles. There were 93 runners remaining when they left Glenrio on April 4. The runners endured snow and sleet during much of the six-day journey across the Panhandle and the mud of the Jericho Gap caused several injuries. Andy Payne, a part Cherokee from the Route 66 town of Foyil, Oklahoma, won the race. Pyle lost a pile of money, but Route 66 was front-page news.

Since the major cities of Texas were far to the south, there was little interest in improving Route 66. A dirt section between Alanreed and Groom became infamous as the Jericho Gap, where thick mud trapped vehicles. The route across the state was not fully paved until 1937.

Images of overloaded jalopies and choking clouds of dust will forever be associated with Route 66 during the Great Depression. In *The Grapes of Wrath*, John Steinbeck called Route 66 "The Mother Road, the road of flight." But Route 66 provided an economic lifeline for those who remained behind, and government relief programs put men to work paving the Jericho Gap.

During World War II, leisure travel slowed dramatically, and the 66 Highway Association disbanded. But another great migration took place as families headed west to seek jobs at defense plants and facilities like the Pantex Plant and the Amarillo Army Airfield.

In 1946, Nat King Cole recorded Bobby Troup's anthem "Get Your Kicks on Route 66," firmly establishing the route in pop culture. Tourist attractions and motels with Native American and Western imagery sprang up on the roadside, especially on the east end of Amarillo.

Even during the glory days, change was in the air. The popularity of Route 66 was proving to be its undoing. In 1947, the US Highway 66 Association was reorganized and could boast 66 had "800 miles of 4-lane highway." But the section of two-lane between Shamrock and Amarillo became known as "Bloody 66."

The state of Texas made up for its previous lax attitude after World War II, and by 1947, work in Texas accounted for 25 percent of all highway construction in the United States. Route 66 had been improved to four lanes from the Oklahoma line almost to Groom and from Amarillo to Bushland by 1954.

Inspired by the autobahns of Germany he saw during World War II, Pres. Dwight Eisenhower signed the Interstate Highway Act in 1956, providing federal money for a new system of superhighways. Interstate 40 would replace Route 66 across the Panhandle.

Route 66 continued to hold allure even while it was being replaced. From 1960 to 1964, the CBS television series *Route 66* followed Tod Stiles (Courtesy of Martin Milner) and Buzz Murdock (George Maharis) as they found adventure in their Corvette.

In 1962, the US Highway 66 Association met in Shamrock and passed a resolution asking highway officials to name the new route between Chicago and Los Angeles Interstate 66. But the bureaucrats refused. By the 1970s, most of the Mother Road had been replaced by portions of five interstates across the country, I-55, I-44, I-40, I-15, and I-10.

Route 66 held on a little longer in Texas because much of Interstate 40 used portions of the route to save construction costs and because of resistance by communities and business owners. It would be 1984 before McLean became the last community in Texas and the second to last in the nation to be bypassed. Route 66 was decommissioned in 1985.

But the old road would not die. Travelers from all over the world still seek out the old motels, diners, and tourist traps along the Main Street of America. Route 66 is for those who think that the journey is as important as the destination. There is not much to see blasting across Texas on Interstate 40 at 75 miles per hour. The adventure is waiting at the next off ramp.

One

Wheeler County

Route 66 travelers crossing into Texas from Oklahoma once passed this Art Deco–style granite monument. It was erected as part of several highway improvement projects begun in 1934 and slated for completion before the Texas Centennial celebration in 1936. This structure had disappeared by the 1950s, replaced by one of the familiar Texas-shaped stone monuments. (Courtesy of Texas Department of Transportation.)

This 1957 photograph faces west, entering Texas from Oklahoma on the new four-lane Route 66. Note the Texas-shaped monument in the background. Just out of the frame was a sign erected in June 1952, dedicating Route 66 as the Will Rogers Highway. The sign later disappeared, but it was replaced by a beautiful granite marker in 2002.

Many businesses along Route 66 sold cartoon postcards like this one poking fun at some stereotypical images of the Texas roadside. They were part of a series created by Amarillo cartoonist Glenn Zulauf for the Baxter Lane Company and could be customized with the name of the business.

The flat terrain across Texas requires few bridges. This one, eight miles east of Shamrock, is unusual because it originally had two decks to carry 66 and the now abandoned Chicago, Rock Island & Gulf Railroad. The steel beams were encased in concrete to avoid damage from the smoke-belching locomotives. There are no bridges on Interstate 40, just a few feet away. Those bridges were dismantled and the gully was filled in when the railroad tracks were removed.

Route 66 motorists were welcomed at this Colonial-style information center, opened by the Texas Highway Department at Shamrock in 1938. Shamrock was named by Irish immigrant George Nickel in 1890, when he sought to open a post office at his dugout home. Nickel's post office was never built, but the railroad named the stop Shamrock when the town was laid out in 1902. (Courtesy of Texas Department of Transportation.)

Shamrock's most famous landmark is the Tower station and U-Drop Inn Café, constructed by John Tindall and R.C. Lewis. Using a rusty nail, John Nunn is said to have scratched out the design in the dusty driveway of the Crossroads Motor Court across the highway. Tindall hired architect R.C. Berry to complete his vision, and the $29,000 building opened on April 1, 1936. Nunn and his wife, Bebe, would run the café in the station's annex. (Courtesy of Steve Rider.)

Tower Station was called "the most up to date edifice of its kind on US Highway 66 between Oklahoma City and Amarillo." A local youth won $50 for suggesting the name U-Drop Inn for the café. The Nunns sold it after a few years, but returned in 1950, and it became Nunn's Café. Grace Brunner took over in 1957, and changed the name to the Tower Café. By 1976, the station had been rebranded as Fina and was painted red, white, and blue.

James R. Tindall, whose father built the Tower station, took over in the 1980s. He restored the original colors and brought back the name U-Drop Inn. The U-Drop Inn closed in 1995, but the bank that owned the building deeded it to the city, which turned it into a visitor center. The U-Drop Inn and its amazing neon was the inspiration for Ramone's House of Body Art in fictional Radiator Springs, the setting for the 2006 Pixar animated film *Cars*.

Shamrock is extremely proud of its Irish heritage. In 1938 the town bandmaster, Glenn Truax, started the tradition of a big parade and celebration to mark St. Patrick's Day. Every year, the men in Shamrock dye their beards green. In 1959, Shamrock acquired a piece of the famous Blarney Stone from Blarney Castle in County Cork, Ireland. The stone can be found in Elmore Park.

Two major Shamrock landmarks are the Texas Theatre and the water tower, both visible on the right. There were once 41 theaters across the state bearing the name Texas, but the one in Shamrock is the last still showing films. The 176-foot-tall Shamrock water tower is billed as the tallest of its type in Texas, and a plaza beneath the tower features displays showing its construction.

This 1950s photograph looks west on Route 66 from the junction with US 83 during the heyday of Shamrock. Mr. and Mrs. W.L. Jacobs' gift shop and Standard Service is at right. The pumps there were once sheltered from the hot Texas sun by a huge awning. The site is a vacant lot today. Most of these businesses closed or moved when Interstate 40 opened in 1973.

John Sheerin incorporated the Shamrock Oil and Gas Company in 1929 and named it after a symbol of his native Ireland. Shamrock was originally headquartered in Amarillo, and the stations were common across nine states. Shamrock merged with Diamond Alkali in 1967 to form Diamond-Shamrock, which became a division of Valero Energy Corporation. (Courtesy of Steve Rider.)

It was a big day at Oscar B. Luman's Mobil station when the 1962 Mobil Economy Run pulled in to fuel up. From 1936 to 1968, except during World War II, the runs were held annually to determine fuel economy statistics for various classes of automobiles. Luman originally owned a station on Route 66 in Erick, Oklahoma, before coming to Shamrock in 1958. (Courtesy of Devil's Rope Museum.)

The office and cabins at the 14-unit Village Motel featured beautiful rock exteriors and a nice playground for the children. The complex still stands, next door to the former Clay Motor Company, which served Route 66 travelers from 1947 to 2013. Clay Motors was once an Edsel dealership; a graveyard of junked Edsels is across the highway.

Shamrock Court, advertised as "Shamrock's Largest and Finest Motor Court," had 24 "modern, quiet air-cooled insulated units, tile baths, tubs and showers" and also boasted "Beauty Rest Beds. Heated by Panelray. Free Garages." Shamrock Court was recommended by Duncan Hines and was a Best Western member motel.

Three distinctive Art Deco stations with crenellations and pylons still stand in Shamrock, including this former Whiting Brothers station built in 1938. Whiting Brothers stations and motels once lined Route 66 from Shamrock to Barstow. This structure became the Sugar Shack Donut and Cappuccino Shop and then Route 66 Truck Parts and Towing.

The 28-unit Sun 'n Sand Motel and the Maverick Restaurant opened in September 1953. The motel used the slogan "We have everything but you." It later became the Sun 'n Sand Motor Inn and was operated by Mr. and Mrs. Chester Glancy Jr., a family that also operated motels on Route 66 in Oklahoma. The motel is still in business as the Route 66 Inn.

Shamrock's motel row once featured roughly a dozen big neon signs, including the one at the Ranger Motel. The Ranger was billed as "Shamrock's Newest and Finest" when this postcard was mailed in 1963. The Ranger, a Best Western motel, featured year-round air conditioning and a heated pool. It survives as the Shamrock Country Inn.

The Rambler Restaurant, the "Home of the Rambler Dressing," was located across Route 66 from the Rambler Motel and was operated by Pearl and Daulton Ford Newkirk. The motel was built by Joe K. Lester and was also operated at one time by Landes and Sally Horton. The Rambler Motel became the Blarney Inn, and the former restaurant building still stands.

Mr. and Mrs. H.G. Tucker operated the Kelly Motel in the early 1960s, calling it "your home away from home." It was owned by Helen and Carrol Williams at the time of this photograph. They advertised that the Kelly Motel was "easy to find—hard to leave," and featured "tastefully furnished rooms." The units still stand adjacent to the Texas Motel.

Bennie and Eunice Schlegel are shown here outside their Sun Tan Motel on the west side of Shamrock. This motel had an ultra-modern design featuring a glassed-in lobby. It had 16 rooms that started at $4 per night, with television included. The glass that gave the motel its distinctive look has mostly been covered up, and it is now the deteriorating Texas Motel. (Courtesy of Devil's Rope Museum.)

The high plains of the Panhandle are sometimes called the "Golden Spread of Texas." The term originated with an Amarillo radio announcer and has been used to promote tourism. The word "Golden" is said to symbolize the sunny climate, and of course, "Spread" comes from the massive ranches of the Panhandle. Several businesses in the Amarillo area use the name.

In his *Guide Book to Highway 66*, published in 1946, Jack Rittenhouse wrote that Lela had five service stations, a café, and a post office. Mostly ruins remain today. The town was known as "Story" when originally established as a railroad stop. But postmaster Bedford F. Bowers renamed it after his sister-in-law in 1903. The high school closed in 1992.

E. Mike Allred was a gruff former carnival man who had operated a notorious snake pit on Route 66 in Elk City, Oklahoma, before bringing his slithery friends to Alanreed. At first, he partnered with his sister Addie, but the two clashed. Alone, he established the Regal Reptile Ranch in an old gas station (with a huge neon steer on top) west of Lela. (Courtesy of Devil's Rope Museum.)

E. Mike was also known for breeding and displaying his "Supernatural Raccoons" with glowing eyes. Only a few scattered boards remain on the site, but the former gas station (minus the neon steer) survives today along Route 66 as part of the Red River Steakhouse in McLean. (Courtesy of Red River Steakhouse.)

This sign on four-lane Route 66/Interstate 40 advertised the Regal Reptile Ranch. E. Mike Allred died in 1979, and his sister Addie returned and ran the ranch until it closed in the 1980s. The big sign blew down during a storm in 2007 and was partially reconstructed in town.

Two

Gray County

During World War II, up to 3,000 German prisoners of war at a time were housed at the McLean Permanent Internment Camp. Pfc. Clawson L. Leavitt is shown in this photograph serving as an MP at the camp, which some locals called the "Fritz Ritz." Prisoners who chose to work made 80¢ per day, and most were well behaved. Two prisoners were executed for unknown offenses, and two tried to escape. They got lost and surrendered to a startled rancher. The entrance was off Route 66 at County Line Road, and the camp closed on July 6, 1945. (Courtesy of Deanna Boddicker.)

This intersection five miles east of McLean was known as Jones Corner, after Zack and Nora Jones. Their station also served as a post office and was a popular place for off-duty soldiers stationed at the POW camp. That could have been because Zack and his wife, Flora, had six beautiful daughters. The station, later operated by James Chastain, was torn down when Route 66 was widened. (Courtesy of Steve Rider.)

The owner of the massive R.O. Ranch, Alfred Rowe, donated the land for the town of McLean, laid out around a railroad cattle shipping point. Rowe moved back to his native England in 1910 and was making a trip to check on the ranch when he booked passage on the *Titanic*. He is said to have been found atop an iceberg, frozen to death, with his gold watch still ticking.

The marker in this photograph, which read "McLean" on the other side, was sponsored by the Lions Club and erected about the time Route 66 was paved in 1933. The route originally followed First Street. In 1951, Route 66 was divided through town, with eastbound traffic using Railroad Avenue and westbound 66 following First Street. In July 1984, McLean became the last town in Texas bypassed by Interstate 40. (Courtesy of Texas Department of Transportation.)

Much of McLean's commercial district remains intact, and is listed in the National Register of Historic Places. The structure shown here during an April snowstorm in 1938 was constructed by Fred O'Dell in 1914 as the O'Dell Hotel. In 1916, J.R. and Mary Hindman took over, and it became the Hindman Hotel. The building was barely standing in 2013. (Courtesy of Devil's Rope Museum.)

The Avalon Theatre was originally owned and operated by Mr. and Mrs. Edgar Adams and opened on March 26, 1936, showing the film *Follow the Fleet*, starring Fred Astaire and Ginger Rogers. It closed in the 1980s, and the beautiful Art Deco facade was later restored by the Old Route 66 Association of Texas.

Two huge balls of barbed wire stand in front of the Devil's Rope and Old Route 66 Museum in McLean. Inside are barbed wire sculptures, tools, and displays of military "war wire." In 1874, Joseph Glidden patented barbed wire as we know it, referred to by the Indians as "Devil's Rope." His partner Henry B. Sanborn, "The Father of Amarillo" introduced barbed wire to the Panhandle.

The big, yellow welded cobra that once loomed outside E. Mike Allred's Regal Reptile Ranch now resides in the Old Route 66 section of the Devil's Rope Museum. Other displays include the original plastic steer that once stood in front of the Big Texan Restaurant in Amarillo. Delbert and Ruth Trew opened the museum in an old brassiere factory on March 21, 1991.

There were once 22 auto-related businesses in McLean. The McLean Filling Station was a rival of the garage and station operated by Harris D'Spain and his brother Ancil. Their station changed locations and names several times, and at least four of the six D'Spain brothers were involved with the business at some point. (Courtesy of Devil's Rope Museum.)

Odell Fosque Mantooth operated his station at 119 East First Street from 1945 until he died in 1981. He was a very active member of the Highway 66 Association and fought against Interstate 40. As a city councilman, Mantooth helped reshape the image of McLean as the "Uplift City." The old station is vacant but still stands. (Courtesy of Devil's Rope Museum.)

Grace Bruner's Greyhound Drug served as the McLean bus station and was very popular with the teenagers. There was no cafeteria at the school, so Grace opened a lunch counter downstairs to serve the kids. She called it the Tiger's Den and even provided comic books and music. Grace also operated the Tower Café and Greyhound Station at the U-Drop Inn. (Courtesy of Devil's Rope Museum.)

The first Phillips 66 station in Texas opened in McLean in 1929 and was operated by Charles Weaver from 1959 until it closed in 1977. Early Phillips 66 stations used a Tudor-style cottage design and were painted dark green with orange and blue trim to stand out from competitors. The Old Route 66 Association of Texas restored the exterior of this station in 1992.

Raymond Guyton worked in the oil fields before coming to McLean in 1950 and opening Guyton Motors with his wife, Lorene. Route 66 once provided enough business for Guyton's wrecker and mechanic service to operate around the clock. Guyton also offered body work and ran a used car lot on the site. The building has been vacant since he died in 1998.

This billboard, highlighting some of the local industries (including the bra factory), stood on four-lane Route 66 entering McLean from the west. The bra factory made McLean the "Uplift Capitol of the World." It closed down in 1970. The old factory now houses the Devil's Rope and Old Route 66 Museum, the first museum with a Route 66 theme.

"Slim" Windom drove a dump truck during construction of Route 66 in the infamous Jericho Gap. In 1951, he opened the West Wind Motel with his wife, Grace. They later built the Windi Inn on a high hill along the new four-lane Route 66 west of Alanreed. The West Wind became the Cactus Motel in the 1960s. As of 2013, it is still in business and is operated by Peggy Baer, the mayor of McLean.

Alanreed had been known as "Spring Tank," "Gouge Eye," and "Prairie Dog Town" before residents named it after the railroad contracting firm Alan and Reed. Alanreed is the home of the oldest church and cemetery on Route 66 in Texas. The First Baptist Church, shown here, was constructed in 1904, and the first burial at the cemetery was in 1890.

The Old Route 66 Association of Texas restored Bradley Kiser's 66 Super Service Station, opened in 1930. The Standish Courts, located nearby, were also a stop in Alanreed. In February 1956, three people died at the tourist court after drinking a mixture of antifreeze, hair tonic, and bay rum. They had rigged a still in their room to boil down the antifreeze.

Three

Donley and Carson Counties

The Jericho Gap, 17 miles of dirt road between Alanreed and Groom, was the most notorious segment of Route 66. Vehicles became hopelessly bogged down in the gooey mud and it was rumored that locals watered down the road to make money pulling cars from the muck. A gravel road opened on January 13, 1934, and an asphalt surface was ready on September 15, 1936. On October 9, over 3,000 people gathered in McLean to celebrate. (Courtesy of Nick Gerlich.)

The competitors in the epic 1928 footrace across America dubbed the "Bunion Derby" battled cold, sleet, and injuries due to the muddy roads as they crossed the Jericho Gap. Several of the vehicles carrying supplies were stuck in the mud for hours, and a storm cancelled the festivities in Amarillo. Andy Payne, no. 43, moved into first place as the runners crossed into his home state of Oklahoma on April 8. He went on to win the race. (Courtesy of El Reno Carnegie Library.)

Sections of the Jericho Gap can be driven, but only if the weather is dry. The crumbling ruins of a tourist court and a fallen windmill are all that remain in Jericho today. To reach the Jericho Gap, take Interstate 40 exit 124 and turn south for one mile to Dirt 66, now County Road B. This road still turns into a quagmire when wet.

The new road north of Jericho eliminated the dreaded gap. But the narrow, two-lane highway still earned the nickname "Bloody 66." Commenting on the nearly two dozen deaths between Amarillo and Shamrock in 1941, the Amarillo newspaper reported that nearly every deadly crash involved at least one vehicle from California. (Courtesy of Texas Department of Transportation.)

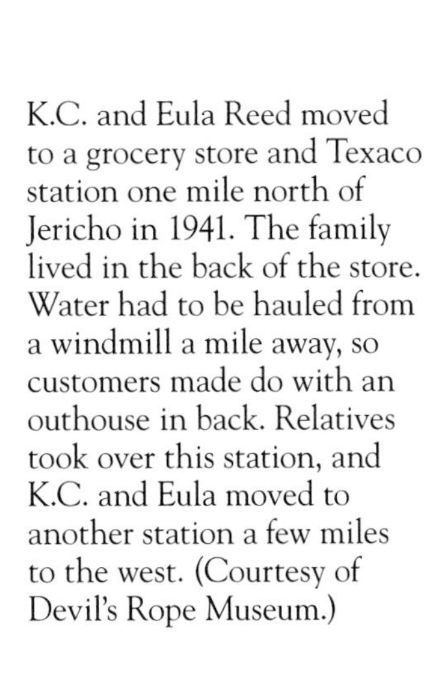

K.C. and Eula Reed moved to a grocery store and Texaco station one mile north of Jericho in 1941. The family lived in the back of the store. Water had to be hauled from a windmill a mile away, so customers made do with an outhouse in back. Relatives took over this station, and K.C. and Eula moved to another station a few miles to the west. (Courtesy of Devil's Rope Museum.)

K.C. Reed died in 1948 and is buried in the Jericho cemetery. Eula continued with the business and was able to add running water and a bathroom in 1948. She had a new station and home built in 1956–1957. Eula died at age 87 in 1979. K.C. and Eula's son John opened this Gulf station at Groom in 1951 and continued in the business until 1966. (Courtesy of Devil's Rope Museum.)

The four-lane divided roadway between Alanreed and Groom reduced the carnage on "Bloody 66" when it opened in 1953. But there were also many serious accidents due to the increased speeds. Much of Route 66 in this area was used for Interstate 40 to save construction costs and was not upgraded to full freeway standards until 1980. (Courtesy of Texas Department of Transportation.)

During the 1950s, the Texas Highway Department began constructing modern Safety Rest Areas, such as this one along four-lane Route 66 just west of Alanreed. A sturdy canopy protected the picnic tables, and several of these shelters are still in use along the sections of Interstate 40 that follow the old alignment of Route 66. (Courtesy of Texas Department of Transportation.)

The design of the modern Donley County Route 66 Safety Rest Area was inspired by the 66 Motel in Groom. The rest area, accessible from eastbound Interstate 40 west of Alanreed, contains exhibits and computer displays highlighting the history of Route 66, Route 66 mosaics in the restrooms, and a Route 66–themed playground. It opened in 2003.

Groom, another railroad stop laid out in 1902, was named for cattleman Col. B.B. Groom, general manager of the Francklyn Land and Cattle Company. His extravagance bankrupted the firm, but the colonel was the first to hire men to drill wells to provide water for cattle. The town thrived on Route 66 business until Interstate 40 opened on June 2, 1980. (Courtesy of David Eppen.)

The 66 Courts in Groom opened in 1947 and included a café and gas station. It fell into ruins after Interstate 40 arrived. A vintage bullet-riddled Edsel out front made the scene a favorite for photographers. But the station and garage was torn down in 2004 and the motel came down in 2005. The sign survives today at the Roadhouse 66 Bar and Grill in Columbus, Ohio.

Pete Ford built the Golden Spread Motel in 1953. In 1992, the director of *Leap of Faith*, starring Steve Martin, wanted to use it for the movie but the owner turned him down. The director bought another motel in town, and then added a second story and a sign to make it look just like the Golden Spread. The motel closed in 1987 and is now a storage business.

Paul Homer was a butcher at the Groom Produce and Market for 20 years before he bought an old Sinclair station and cafe on Route 66 and Martin Avenue. When Route 66 was widened in 1955, he moved the café and built a new station. It became Homer's Magnolia Service, later expanded to become Homer's Mobil Service. Homer retired in 1971. (Courtesy of Devil's Rope Museum.)

Ruby Denton ran the Golden Spread Grill in Groom from 1957 to 2002. Known for Ruby's cinnamon rolls, steak sandwiches, and hamburgers, the grill advertised: "Always stop at the Golden Spread and be among the best fed." Ruby died in December 2011 at age 90. The building now houses the Route 66 Steakhouse.

Even though the weather gets rough in the Panhandle, this leaning water tower at Groom was not damaged in a tornado. It was built that way to promote Ralph Britten's Truck Stop, long since closed. Another roadside landmark beckons just to the west. The 190-foot-tall Cross of Our Lord Jesus Christ Ministries is the second largest in the western hemisphere.

There once was enough traffic to support four restaurants in Groom, including the Ranch House Café. It was owned by Jimmie and Mamie McCasland and later by Jim Littlefield, who advertised the "Best Coffee in Texas." Jim and Carolyn Moraniec now run the Blessed Mary Café here. There is no cash register and no prices are on the menu, only a sign asking diners to "pay what you can." Any profits are donated to charity.

Former trucker Jack West and his wife Bettye took over the Groom Truck Stop on May 15, 1962, and it was open around the clock until May 15, 1982. According to Jack, Elvis Presley stopped here several times in the early 1970s because the King did not like the crowds in Amarillo. The building still stands with a shattered sign and a lot filled with junk. (Courtesy of *Route 66 Magazine* Collection.)

This Route 66 traveler was photographed in 1957 at the intersection with FM 294 just west of Groom. In his 1946 *Guide Book to Highway 66*, Jack Rittenhouse wrote: "Continuing on a treeless, flat plain, US 66 lies straight as a dropped arrow" west of Groom as it approached the tiny hamlet of Lark, named for rancher Lark Stangler. Lark had a population of about 10 and had faded away by the Interstate era.

The Chicago, Rock Island & Pacific Railroad put down tracks and laid out stations across the Panhandle in 1902–1903 and Route 66 followed the rail line much of the way. The CRI&P merged with the reorganized Rock Island in 1948. The steam engine shown here west of Groom was probably replaced by a diesel engine within a few years. The line was abandoned in the 1980s. (Courtesy of David Eppen.)

Cecil and Zelma Walker operated the Phillips 66 station in Conway, the last stop for gas before Amarillo, 25 miles away. Conway traces its roots to the Lone Star School, established in 1892 and the first successful rural school in the Panhandle. The town was laid out in 1903 after the railroad arrived and the one-room school was moved there. (Courtesy of Devil's Rope Museum.)

The best-preserved stretch of original Route 66 in Texas runs west of Conway for a little over seven miles to Interstate 40. It seems nearly as isolated today as when this photograph was taken following a 1938 snowstorm. The original dirt alignment continued west where FM 2161 now angles north and then followed a zigzag pattern to Washburn, joining present-day US 287. Some sources report incorrectly that 66 went through Claude. (Courtesy of Texas Department of Transportation.)

Route 66 will forever be linked with images of refugees fleeing the Dust Bowl of the 1930s. The hardest-hit area included the Texas Panhandle, where Arthur Rothstein photographed this car fleeing one of the "black blizzards." The Panhandle endured 192 "dusters" between 1933 and 1936. About 35 percent of the farmers in the region left between 1935 and 1937. (Courtesy of Library of Congress.)

Tom Crutchfield's family operated the Longhorn Trading Post and a service station on the south side of Interstate 40 at Exit 96. Hoping to attract more business, Tom created a parody of the famous Cadillac Ranch by planting five Volkswagen "Bugs" in the ground. The businesses closed anyway in 2003, but the Bug Ranch still draws people toting cans of spray paint.

Four

Amarillo Area

Many interesting people traveled Route 66 across Texas. Ivan Shockey, the "Sunshine Kid from the Sunshine State" is shown in Amarillo during his nearly three-month journey by burro cart from Santa Fe, New Mexico, to the Century of Progress Exposition at Chicago. Shockey made his 1934 trip to promote tourism and raised money by signing autographs. He was nearly killed by a hit-and-run driver on Route 66 in Illinois. (Courtesy of Steve Rider.)

Painter Georgia O'Keefe described Palo Duro Canyon southeast of Amarillo as "a burning, seething cauldron, filled with dramatic light and color." Formed by the Prairie Dog Town Fork of the Red River, the "Grand Canyon of Texas" is 120 miles long and up to 950 feet deep. The state of Texas and the Civilian Conservation Corps developed the site for Palo Duro Canyon State Park, which opened on July 4, 1934.

Paul Green's musical drama *Texas* has been presented during the summer at the outdoor Pioneer Amphitheatre at Palo Duro Canyon since 1966. The spectacular production opens with a lone rider carrying a Texas flag on the rim of the cliff, 600 feet above the stage. Then a cast of over 60 performers and dramatic effects tell the story of the West Texas settlers.

The Sad Monkey Railroad was once a big attraction at Palo Duro Canyon and was named for a nearby rock formation. The tracks for the miniature railroad were removed in 1996, but visitors can still follow much of the old route on a covered wagon ride. The engine resides in front of a ranch headquarters on Highway 217 a few miles west of the park entrance. The girl is Janice Simpson. (Courtesy of Carl Simpson.)

Ranching in the Panhandle began when Charles Goodnight and John Adair drove a herd of longhorn into Palo Duro Canyon in 1876 and established the JA Ranch. Goodnight is credited with inventing the chuck wagon, and the movie *Lonesome Dove* was loosely based on his life. Other vast Panhandle spreads included the Frying Pan, and the LX Ranch near Amarillo. The XIT Ranch was the largest by far, covering three million acres and parts of 10 counties. (Courtesy of Library of Congress.)

Amarillo was actually founded twice. In 1887, James Berry laid out the town of Oneida near a railroad construction camp known as "Ragtown." Oneida became the county seat and soon took the name of the nearby creek surrounded by yellow soil. Amarillo is Spanish for "yellow." In June 1888 Henry B. Sanborn, the "Father of Amarillo," began buying up land on higher ground a mile east of town.

An 1889 flood convinced most Amarillo residents to move to Henry Sanborn's addition. The county seat was moved in 1893, and Amarillo became a major cattle-shipping center with a population of "500-600 humans and 50,000 head of cattle." More humans moved in after the discovery of natural gas in 1918 and oil in 1921. There are still plenty of cattle too. The skyline is shown here in 1975.

The first automobile in Amarillo arrived in 1903. It was a one-cylinder Cadillac purchased by Dr. W.A. Lockett. Saloon patrons would run outside to hold their jittery mounts as the noisy contraption approached. Ernest Thompson ran this early dealership. General Thompson served as mayor from 1929 to 1932 and became a world leader in petroleum conservation.

Twice a month between 1905 and 1910, a herd of automobiles traveled over the grassy prairie near Amarillo. The Santa Fe Railroad offered reduced rates for these regular "Homeseekers" excursions. The railroad passengers were met by developers, realtors, and promoters in a caravan of touring cars. The excursions helped settle the vast ranch and farmlands of the Panhandle.

The intersection of US 66 and 60 formed a triangle, where former Borger, Texas, mayor S.M. Clayton opened the Triangle Motel (left) in 1946. The motel suffered when the highway was cut off by the new runway at Amarillo Air Force Base in 1955, and then again in 1968, when the base closed and Interstate 40 opened to traffic. The Triangle closed in 1977, but Alan McNeil has been working on restoration. (Courtesy of Texas Department of Transportation.)

The Bell Motel at 7507 Northeast Eighth Avenue, now Amarillo Boulevard, advertised a long list of amenities such as "television, panel ray heat, refrigerated air conditioning, wall to wall carpeting, and a playground for the kiddies." There were many more extras such as "tile showers and Franciscan furniture, all at reasonable rates."

Vol's Restaurant was operated by Vol McClanahan, who also owned a couple of other restaurants in Amarillo. The interior resembled a barn, and was decorated with old saddles and other antiques. They offered "soft organ music" along with the finest in foods. The restaurant at 7505 Northeast Eighth Avenue was destroyed by fire on November 5, 1961.

Vol McClanahan decided his new restaurant would resemble a barn inside and out, and the Country Barn opened in December 1962. John Marrs and his family ran it for many years beginning in 1964. They moved to a new location on Interstate 40, shown here, in 1974. The Country Barn is now known for Bonsmara beef and a classic Cadillac hanging on the bar wall.

Prairie Dog Town, opened in 1954, was a village of tiny buildings and prairie dog burrows designed to draw travelers to the curio shop at 5901 Northeast Eighth Avenue. "Mayor" Forrest "Fist" Ansley, shown here, once owned the Bungalow Courts and was president of the National US Highway 66 Association from 1950 to 1951. The site is still said to be infested with prairie dogs.

Harold English established an airfield east of the original Municipal Airport in 1929. English Field became the Amarillo Air Terminal in 1952 and Amarillo International Airport in 1976. This terminal stands empty, replaced in 1971. In 2003, the airport was named for astronaut Richard Husband, who died aboard the space shuttle *Columbia*. The runway built by the Strategic Air Command in the 1950s is now the third longest commercial runway in the world.

The Aviatrix Club across from Amarillo's original municipal airport was named in honor of Amelia Earhart. She had often stopped in for a steak after buzzing the place. After World War II, Carlton Scales greatly expanded it into the Aviatrix Ballroom, which hosted artists such as Buddy Holly, Louis Armstrong, and Duke Ellington. The original building burned in the 1950s and the Aviatrix closed on August 5, 1989. Only a rusty old "A" still stands atop the sign.

The Army established the Amarillo Air Field next to English Field in April 1942. The 1,523-acre base was used to train pilots, crewmen, and mechanics for B-17 bombers. Training to service the big B-29s was instituted later. Amarillo Air Field closed on September 15, 1946. The nearby Pantex Army Ordnance Plant was also a vital defense installation.

In 1950, the old Amarillo Air Field was reactivated as Amarillo Air Base. The base covered over 5,000 acres, housed a wing of the Strategic Air Command, and accommodated 25,000 airmen at the height of the Cold War. It became the 330th Basic Military School in 1966 and closed in December 1968, a sharp blow to the local economy.

Minnie Ruth Connor opened her first steakhouse in 1950 next to the Trail Drive-In and later moved to this location at 5106 Northeast Eighth Avenue, across from the Aviatrix Club. Ruth can be seen in the far left corner, posing behind the bar with her grandson. Ruth's was especially known for rib-eye steaks; it closed in 1978. Ruth died in 1997 and the building later became the Thai House.

Keith Applegate's Colonial Courts at 5407 Northeast Eighth Avenue was one of the first motels westbound travelers on Route 66 encountered on the motel row. It was also a favorite with military families and visitors to Amarillo Air Force Base. It later became the Colonial Manor, operated by Clinton and Eva Lowe, and is now the Rama Motel.

The Eastridge Bowling Palace, "the most modern and up-to-date in the Southwest," officially opened at 5405 Northeast Eighth Avenue on November 21, 1959, and was originally managed by John Hathcock. It advertised 32 lanes, free nursery service, and a fine restaurant with an all-electric kitchen. It is now Eastridge Lanes, and the vintage sign remains.

Tommy Petropoulis operated Pete and Sons Place at 5009 Northeast Eighth Avenue. He advertised "baked ham and steaks" as their specialty and offered the "best coffee on this highway" for 5¢. The family also operated a trucking business. The café became the Restaurante Los Hermanos Ramirez, and the truck stop portion housed an auto repair business as of 2013. (Courtesy of Steve Rider.)

Florence "Ma" Madsen's dining room at 4800 Northeast Eighth Street was famous for fried chicken and opened in 1938. It was a tradition here for diners to pin their business cards over their hometown on a big wall map of the United States. Ma sold in 1944, and it became the Thomas Dinner House. The site is now occupied by a mobile and prefab home sales lot.

The Biltmore Courts at 4600 Northeast Eighth Avenue opened in the spring of 1945 and was operated for many years by Alford Tedford. The court was advertised as "only nine minutes from downtown." A "noted reader and advisor," Madame O'Malley operated out of a cottage here during the 1950s. It later became the Woods Inn, and the site is now a mobile home dealership. (Courtesy of Steve Rider.)

Underwood's Bar-B-Q began serving its famous hickory-smoked meats in Amarillo at 4513 Northeast Eighth Avenue in 1956. It was originally managed by Don Rappe. Underwood's later moved to 301 West Amarillo Boulevard but closed in 1978. This building later became the first home of the Big Texan and was occupied by a mobile home supply store in 2013.

When R.J. "Bob" Lee returned to his hometown in 1959, he was disappointed to find there was no restaurant that captured the flavor of the "Old West." In 1960, he opened the Big Texan at the former Underwood's Bar-B-Q location at 4513 Northeast Eighth Avenue. In 1962, he began a promotion offering a free 72-ounce steak dinner if eaten in one hour.

Bob Lee is on the left in this photograph with Big Texan public relations man Chuck Gallimore. The 72-ounce steak dinner also includes a salad, baked potato, and shrimp cocktail. Competitive eater Joey Chestnut set the current record in 2008, polishing it all off in eight minutes and 52 seconds. Klondike Bill, a 368-pound wrestler, ate two in one hour in the 1960s.

The 72-ounce steak promotion made the Big Texan famous, but business plummeted after Interstate 40 opened on November 15, 1968, and Bob moved the restaurant to this location on the new highway in 1970. He used lumber salvaged from the barracks at Amarillo Air Force Base for the new building, which burned on July 13, 1976, but was quickly rebuilt. Bob Lee died in 1990 but the Big Texan is still one of the most popular stops for Route 66 travelers.

Many Route 66 motels, such as the Silver Spur, used Western imagery to attract business. The motel at 4011 Northeast Eighth Avenue also advertised Franciscan Furniture. It was owned by L.V. Stafford, and later by Mansell and Allene McNew. The vintage, boot-shaped sign is still a good place for a photo op, but the motel has seriously deteriorated.

The Capitol Garage and Service Station at 3815 Northeast Eighth Avenue was notable for the rotating neon imitation oil derrick on the roof. The garage, service station, and small café opened about 1940 and was owned by Cleo Scamahorn. Jerry and Jim Hodge operated it from 1949 to 1952, and Oscar Rawlins later took over. The landmark was demolished in 1980. (Courtesy of Steve Rider.)

The vintage signs at the Cattleman's Club and the Cowboy Motel are also excellent photo ops. The motel was originally named Del Camino (Spanish for "the road") and was operated by the Ware family. The Cattleman's Club opened in 1961 and the popular bar and dance hall has been owned by Jeanie Campbell for over 30 years.

The Estess Motel is still in business today at 3511 Northeast Eighth Avenue. It was originally known as Woody's Motel, operated by Schuyler Woody, who also built the Palo Duro Motel. It later became Hill's Motel. Morris and Lena Estess, shown here, took over in the mid-1960s. Morris died in 1967, but Lena lived to be 102, passing away in 2007. (Courtesy of Steve Rider.)

A vacant lot next to Lluvia Imports marks the former site of the Forest Hill Court, 3405 Northeast Eighth Avenue. The 15-unit court was constructed in 1940 by P.M. Johnson, who also operated a grocery store on Route 66. The Forest Hill Court burned in the 1980s. It was promoted on another postcard in conjunction with the Gables Court on Tenth Street, US 287.

Modern accommodations combined with the charm of Pueblo architecture at the Pueblo Motel, 3101 Northeast Eighth Avenue. J. Wilkie Talbert operated the motel, which opened in 1935. Edward Regal ran it from 1947 to 1952. By 1957, it had become the 50-unit Flamingo Motel, and the pueblo look was gone. A carwash occupied the site in 2013. (Courtesy of Lake County Discovery Museum.)

Billed as "the world's largest grain elevators," the 3.3-million-bushel Burris Panhandle Elevators loom over Route 66. The Light Crust Doughboys, a western swing band formed to promote the Burris Mill's Light Crust Flour, were wildly popular during the 1930s and 1940s. Their radio show was heard on over 170 stations. Cargill now owns the elevators. (Courtesy of Library of Congress.)

Barney Toler constructed the Hillcrest Motel at 3017 Northeast Eighth Avenue in 1945. The motel was recommended by AAA and advertised "The best is none too good for our guests." The Hillcrest had 12 units and later expanded to 18 rooms, equipped with "Pulse-A-Rhythm Massage Mats." The Hillcrest Motel is still in operation today.

Opened in 1960, the Hong Kong Restaurant at 3011 Northeast Eighth Avenue was operated by Yim Kwon Jew (pronounced "Joe"). The restaurant advertised "authentic Chinese Cuisine and superb American dishes." It survived the arrival of Interstate 40 and later became the Texas Chicken Bowl. The lower part of the sign has changed, but the dragon is still there.

Bailey's Motel at 2830 Northeast Eighth Avenue opened in 1952 and was operated by James W. Bailey. This colorful postcard noted that it had all tiled baths, tubs, and showers, wall-to-wall-carpets and vented, panel-ray heat. Bailey's later became the Cactus Motel, operated by Ronald Davis, and then developed into the Royal Inn.

A string of brightly lit motels greeted tired travelers at the east end of Amarillo. In 1925, the city directory listed just four "campgrounds." The city also provided a municipal camp that included restrooms and cooking facilities. Just two years later, there were 29 establishments, by then listed as tourist camps. By 1952, there were 68 motels vying for tourist dollars.

Several new motels opened in Amarillo in 1952, including Schuyler Woody's Palo Duro Court, 2820 Northeast Eighth Avenue. The attractive, ranch-style court originally had 20 brick units. It was recommended by AAA and advertised "Amarillo's newest and finest court, offering you distinctive furnishings in a distinctive atmosphere." It is still in business as of 2013.

A.J. Grief opened the True Rest Courts at 2820 Northeast Eighth Avenue in 1941. It originally had 30 modest rooms with garages in between. It was expanded and remodeled in 1954 with a beautiful Spanish Ranch design. Longtime owner Frank Hobgood once served as president of the US 66 Highway Association. The True Rest developed into the Route 66 Inn.

George Pomeroy was also active in the US 66 Highway Association. He operated the 19-unit Redwood Motel, originally known as the Redwood Ranch Motel. It originally had a redwood exterior, which had been covered up by the time this photograph was made. It still stands at 2801 Northeast Eighth Avenue and is now the Redwood Motel and Apartments.

In 1933, there were only nine tourist courts listed on Route 66 in Amarillo, including the Ama-Tone Court, 2417 Northeast Eighth Avenue. Later the Amatone Well Court and Apartments, it was known for its deep well "health water," offered free to all visitors and sold all over the city. The Ama-Tone was also the home of Coffee Pot Bill's Cafe

Joe S. Woon was one of the original owners of the Canton Café in downtown Amarillo. In 1957, he opened the Ding How Restaurant at 2415 Northeast Eighth Avenue. Offering Chinese and American fare, it advertised: "If you eat once at Ding How Restaurant you'll always come back." The shuttered restaurant building and its rusting sign were still standing as of 2013.

The back of this card for the Graycourt Tourist Lodge, opened in the early 1930s at 1706 Northeast Eighth Avenue, touted Amarillo as the Helium City, "Where the Graycourt Tourist Lodge offers strictly modern accommodations at reasonable rates." Later the Graycourt Motel, it was operated by Floyd Verner and then by Thomas J. Braswell. It no longer stands.

The Plainsman Motel opened at 1503 Northeast Eighth Avenue in 1950 with 24 units. In 1959, it was expanded to 120 rooms, and one of the largest motel signs on Route 66 in the Southwest was added. Owners T.M. Montgomery and W.R. Scott dyed the grass green in the winter, and a church group used the pool for baptisms. A supermarket occupies the site today.

The Mary Thomas Restaurant at 1501 Northeast Eighth Avenue is shown here in 1952. The restaurant was advertised as nationally famous for marvelous "Steaks of Distinction" and Tennessee Ham Steaks. Lois Capp owned the restaurant during the 1950s and it became the Phillips Restaurant in 1955. The site is now a supermarket.

Developer Tony Jones opened Amarillo's first Holiday Inn at 1411 Northeast Eighth Avenue in October 1954. It originally had 63 units. L.V. Stafford was the second owner. Lee Stroud of the Park Plaza chain took over in 1957, and another 50 units were added. Stroud owned the Holiday Inns in Amarillo until the Holiday Inns of America corporation took over in 1961.

The Royal Palace Tourist Courts had a distinctive Spanish design and opened in 1938 at 1407 Northeast Eighth Avenue. F.E. Cornelius was the first manager of "One of the finest courts in Texas." It had 18 units and was bringing in $2,000 per month when it was put up for sale in 1946, according to owner Henry L. Ford. The Royal Palace no longer stands.

"Where the North Meets the South," the Minnesota Courts were located at 1107 Northeast Eighth Avenue. Originally known as the Minnesota Motor Courts, the motel was operated by Arthur J. Johnson when this postcard was made in 1952. The postcard notes that it was a five-minute drive to downtown and cites the population of Amarillo as 110,000.

The 140-unit Amarillo Ramada Inn was constructed in 1958 by a group that included television personality George Gobel. A new Ramada Inn opened at Interstate 40 and Nelson in 1976, and this location became La Casa Real and then the Budget Inn before being demolished in 1995. A Sonic drive-in and a carwash now occupy this site. (Courtesy of Mark Potter.)

Owner Dan Thompson decorated the interior of Neal's Charcoal Broiler at 900 Northeast Eighth Avenue with rare guns as well as knick-knacks, like the lock and key from the old Amarillo jail. He traded several guns for a rare painting of Wyatt Earp, displayed at the restaurant. The building later became the Red Steer Restaurant and then a notorious nightclub.

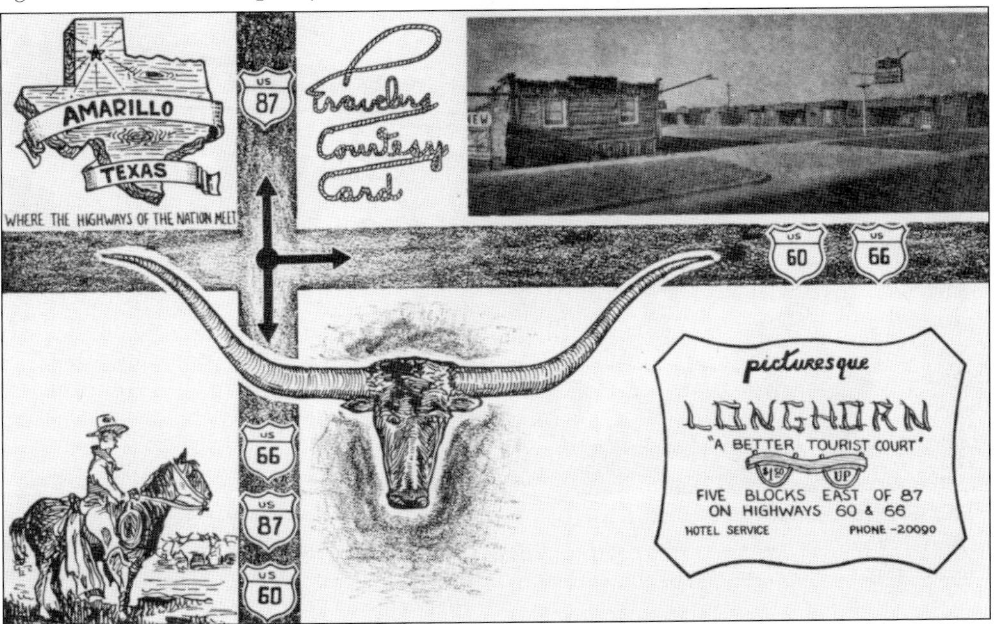

The Longhorn Tourist Court at 801 Northeast Eighth Avenue promoted a western image and a convenient location. It originally featured "Deluxe Log Cabins" and "Little Log Ranch Houses." Later the Longhorn Lodge Motel, it was owned by J.W. Triplett, who formed the Associated Highway Businesses of Amarillo to fight relocation of the highways.

Beef Burger Barrel was originally an A&W Root Beer stand that opened at Tenth Avenue and Polk Street in 1937. F.E. Waller moved it to Northeast Eighth Avenue and Hayes Street in 1947, and the structure was moved to its current location on Plains Boulevard in 1952. The landmark closed in early 2007, but David White reopened it a few months later.

Harry Kindig converted an old gas station at 705 Northeast Eighth Avenue into the Long Champ Dining Salon in 1945. He specialized in seafood but soon learned that the locals preferred steak. Homer and Auline Rice took over in 1947 and changed the name to Rice's Dining Salon in 1953, reportedly after the famous Long Champ Restaurant in New York threatened to sue.

The marquee at Rice's Dining Salon featured over 5,000 bulbs and a leaping neon swordfish at the top. It was said to be the largest restaurant sign between New York and Los Angeles. Homer Rice later opened an adjoining motel that would develop into the Trade Winds East. Homer and Auline retired in 1978, and the building no longer stands.

There were seven Park Plaza Courts across the country, including four spaced about a day's drive apart on Route 66 at St. Louis, Tulsa, Amarillo, and Flagstaff. On June 23, 1949, the nude body of legendary oil well firefighter Tex Thornton was found on a blood-soaked bed in cabin no. 18 at the Amarillo Park Plaza. Thornton had picked up a hitchhiking couple and was killed during a drunken argument over the young lady. The couple was acquitted on the murder charge.

One of the two Toddle Houses in Amarillo was located at 614 Northeast Eighth Avenue, next door to the Park Plaza. It opened in 1955. Toddle House was one of the first franchised restaurants, and specialized in breakfast items. Each one was identical, consisting only of 10 stools at a stainless steel counter. There was no cash register. Diners just placed their payment in a box by the door.

Don D. Parker opened the Grande Tourist Court at 600 Northeast Eighth Avenue in 1937. O.K. "Coe" Dunlap took over the 68-unit complex in 1945. The Grande Court also had an entrance from 720 North Fillmore and was located across from Lincoln Park, which became Will Rogers Memorial Park. The site is now a vacant lot.

A photograph of Grande Court owner O.K. "Cow Waddy" Dunlap astride a pony at his motel was the basis for this postcard, highly sought after by collectors and produced by the Curt Teich Company of Chicago. The touch-up artist added a cowgirl behind Dunlap; a metal eyelet on the card allows her to swing back and forth.

The Western Motel was also located across from the city park at 515 Northeast Eighth Avenue and was advertised as "home owned." Approved by AAA, it had 21 units and boasted a radio in each room. It was later known as Akles Western Motel, the "Home of real Texas hospitality," but no longer stands.

The Jones Brothers Village Restaurant, 413 Northeast Eighth Avenue, was originally the Jones Brothers Drive-In, opened in 1938. It offered "Chicken in the Rough," one of the first franchised foods. Chicken in the Rough was basically a 50¢ chicken dinner eaten without utensils. It was a novel idea at the time, and was introduced by Beverly Osborne at his restaurant on Route 66 in Oklahoma City.

A church designed to resemble the Alamo stood at Northeast Eighth Avenue and Pierce. The First Assembly of God Church was constructed in 1947. Atop the neon sign shaped like a Bible, the cross flashed "Jesus" vertically and "Saves" horizontally. The church was demolished in 1984 to make room for a fast-food restaurant.

La Rose Courts was the first motel located at 317 Northeast Eighth Avenue, "Where the Highways of the Nation Meet." It advertised "A Good Place to Stop. Clean, Modern and Quiet" but was "For Tourists and Commercial Men Only." It had 22 cottages and the structure at left housed the lobby, a reading room, and an additional 12 hotel rooms.

The Sahara Sands Motel took the place of La Rose Courts in 1957. It was advertised as "Amarillo's Outstanding Motel," but the name did not last long. It had become Amarillo's second Holiday Inn by 1959. The sign was sold to Marvin Whittington, owner of the Sahara Sands Motel on Route 66 in Tucumcari, New Mexico.

This little cowgirl posed at Amarillo Boulevard and Fillmore Avenue, the junction of US Highways 60, 66, 87, and 287. Charlotte Lane was four years old when this photograph was taken in 1962. Her father, Lloyd, was a photographer for the postcard company operated by his brother Baxter Lane.

Five

Downtown and West Amarillo

Route 66 originally turned south at Fillmore Street to West Sixth Avenue, veering onto Bushland Boulevard and West Ninth Avenue. In 1953, that route was bypassed in favor of a four-lane extension of Eighth Avenue to the west. The old route became Business 66 and Eighth Avenue became Amarillo Boulevard in 1964. This photograph looks east on Amarillo Boulevard from St. Anthony's Hospital and also shows Bill Gundlach's Texaco station and the Humble (later Enco and then Exxon) station operated by L.G. McKinney.

John Farrell opened the 42-unit Farrell Manor Motel in 1954, and it was remodeled in 1961. The motel and coffee shop were very busy because of the location across from St. Anthony's Hospital. Farrell also built and operated the Manor Bowl and constructed several residential developments. This site later became a parking lot for St. Anthony's new wing.

W.H. Bush donated the site for the first hospital in the Panhandle, and residents raised $1,860 to pay for the construction. The 14-bed St. Anthony's Sanitarium opened on March 28, 1901. In 1928, this grand, five-story building was added, and the name was changed to St. Anthony's Hospital. The original building on the left was demolished in 1955.

A major addition was made at St. Anthony's Hospital in 1960, and it eventually covered six blocks from North Polk Street to Jackson Street and from Eighth Avenue (Amarillo Boulevard) to Northwest Sixth Street. St. Anthony's merged with High Plains Baptist Hospital in 1996 and moved to the Baptist campus on Wallace Boulevard. The last workers left this location in 2004.

The Townhouse Motel still stands on West Amarillo Boulevard at the intersection with Polk Street. Located across from St. Anthony's Hospital, this "beautifully designed motel" advertised: "Everything has been included for your comfort, and the Townhouse Motel is truly your home away from home." It also housed the Top O' Town Restaurant.

The Vic-Mon Motor Hotel opened in 1961 at 601 West Amarillo Boulevard and was named after a famous racehorse. Within a few months, it had become the Holiday Inn West. At one time, there were three Holiday Inns in Amarillo, less than one-and-a-half miles apart on Route 66. The Holiday Inn became the Inn of Amarillo but has since deteriorated.

The Caravan Motel at 620 West Amarillo Boulevard was once an attractive place described by AAA as offering comfortable rooms and a friendly atmosphere. But, by the late 1990s, the motel had deteriorated into a haven for prostitutes and drug dealers and was closed down. It became the Deluxe Motel, but drug raids were still making headlines there in 2012.

The Will Rogers Range Riders is the oldest continuously operated western riding club in the United States and an organization benefitting children's charities. Several Amarillo businessmen founded the group in 1939 and the facilities were located on Amarillo Boulevard near Bell Street, where the highway curved towards the traffic circle. A new arena was built in 2006 on Loop 335.

Back at the intersection with Fillmore Street, 66 travelers could turn north for two blocks and stay at the Bungalow Courts, one of the first tourist courts in Amarillo. It was built at 1004 North Fillmore by J.P. Schreoder in 1927. It advertised: "The experienced traveler stops at the Bungalow Courts, largest for many a mile" and was demolished in 1958.

The Bungalow Courts were demolished for one of the largest motels in the city. The Trade Winds covered the entire 1000 block between North Fillmore Street and North Pierce Street. Constructed and operated by W.T. Smoot Sr. and W.T. Smoot Jr., it had 96 units and was the only motel in Amarillo with two swimming pools.

Actress Lela Mae Teter Barnum gave up the stage to become a housewife. She was awarded half her husband's land when they divorced and became a millionaire when oil was discovered there. In 1926, the "Oil Queen of the Midwest" opened one of the first tourist courts in Amarillo, the Lela Mae Courts at 811 North Fillmore Street. It no longer stands.

Smith's was the first lodging establishment in Amarillo to use the term "motel." It was constructed in 1939 by H.E. Smith at 806 North Fillmore Street (US 87-287) with another entrance from 307 Northeast Eighth Avenue (US 60-66). It was adjacent to a drugstore and Lincoln Park. A small portion, last used as a barbershop, was still standing in 2013.

Amarillo was one of several towns on Route 66 with motels named after the first European explorer of the area, Francisco Vazquez de Coronado. Arthur J. Grief, former owner of the True Rest Courts, operated the Coronado Courts at 705 North Fillmore Street. Grief died in 1947, and the Coronado became the Sun Tan Motel, which no longer stands. (Courtesy of Steve Rider.)

The Silver Grill was a downtown cafeteria billed as Amarillo's largest restaurant. It was originally located on East Third Street next to the Lewis Hotel. Owner Dewey Ashcroft moved it to Fourth Avenue and Polk Street, and it is shown here at its final location, 704 Tyler Street next to the Continental bus station and a block south of Route 66. The Silver Grill closed in 1972.

Bob and Elmer Dowell opened the Saratoga Café at Fourth Avenue and Polk Street in 1948. In 1950, they opened Saratoga Café no. 2 at Fifth Avenue and North Fillmore Street, shown here. Bob Dowell was an avid booster of Route 66 and a pioneer in tourism research. One of his studies showed that drivers traveling north-south had more money and were going from resort to resort, while Route 66 travelers had less money and were going "from kinfolk to kinfolk."

Saratoga Café owner Bob Dowell (center) was a major supporter of women's AAU basketball. His "Dowell's Dolls" team traveled the country decked out in cowboy boots and western wear. At one time, all three of the Dowell brothers, Bob, Elmer and D.A., were running restaurants in Amarillo. Bob Dowell ran for mayor in 1953 and died in March 1992. (Courtesy of Devil's Rope Museum.)

This was one of the rooms with "luxurious furnishings" offered at the 38-unit Elite Courts at 410 North Fillmore Street. The motel owned by Jerl Dewitt advertised: "Where elite tourists gather for modern accommodations" and also included an adjacent trailer court. The Elite fell on hard times when Interstate 40 opened, and was demolished years ago.

This 1937 photograph shows the intersection of US 60, 66, 87, and 287 at Sixth Avenue and Fillmore Street. The newspaper plant at right produced the *Daily News* in the morning and *Globe* in the afternoon. The *Globe* merged with another afternoon paper in 1951 and became the *Globe-Times*. In 2001, the *Daily News* and *Globe-Times* merged into one morning paper, the *Globe-News*. (Courtesy of Texas Department of Transportation.)

The darkest day of the Dust Bowl years in Amarillo came on Black Sunday, April 14, 1935. A massive dust storm that some thought was the end of the world turned day into night. Arnold Rothstein captured this image of Amarillo during a 1936 duster, with winds strong enough to cause these signs to sway back and forth. (Courtesy of Library of Congress.)

The Santa Fe Railroad was completed to Amarillo in 1908, and the new depot at 401 South Grant Street opened two years later. A second-story hotel was added in 1912. The last passenger train left Amarillo in 1971, and the Santa Fe Depot is now vacant. But as of 2013, it was being considered as a site for a proposed railroad museum. (Courtesy of Museum of the American Railroad.)

The Harvey House dining room at the Santa Fe Depot not only served railroad patrons, but was the most elegant restaurant in town. The famous Harvey Girls waiting on the tables were held to very strict standards, having answered an ad calling for "girls of good character, attractive and intelligent." The Fred Harvey restaurant closed on January 31, 1940.

Engine 5000, nicknamed *Madame Queen*, was the greatest of the Santa Fe locomotives. An engineer named her after a character from the "Amos 'n' Andy" radio show. She was in service from December 1930 until November 1953 and logged 1,750,000 miles. The *Queen* was donated to the city of Amarillo in 1957 and displayed at the Santa Fe station until it was relocated to a small park in 2005. Plans are in motion for a museum building to display the locomotive.

The 14-story, terracotta Santa Fe General Office Building was formally opened on January 18, 1930. The remains of a wooly mammoth were excavated from the basement during construction and placed on display at the Panhandle-Plains Museum in Canyon, Texas. The Santa Fe Building is now restored and houses Potter County government offices.

A Route 66 journey to Amarillo by bus often ended at the Greyhound bus terminal at Ninth Avenue and Tyler Street. The terracotta-covered Streamline Moderne structure opened in 1947. Greyhound moved its operations to the Trailways station in 1987, and this structure housed office space before becoming a sports bar.

Businesswoman and civic leader Melissa Dora Callaway Oliver-Eakle carried a pearl-handled revolver after a kidnapping attempt; she reportedly had more money than all the banks in Amarillo combined. She backed construction of the 10-story Oliver-Eakle Building (center) at Sixth Avenue and Polk Street in 1927. "Amarillo's first skyscraper" became the Barfield Building in 1947.

The demand for hotels was so great during the oil boom that crews labored around the clock to complete the 600-room Herring Hotel. Opened on January 1, 1928, the largest hotel in the region was constructed by Cornelius Taylor Herring, cattle baron, oilman, and banker. The Herring, one block off Route 66, has been vacant since the early 1980s and is awaiting redevelopment.

In the 1940s, the Old Tascosa Room opened in the basement of the Hotel Herring. The "preferred night club for dining, dancing and entertainment" featured 11 Western themed frescos by renowned Amarillo artist Harold Dow Bugbee. It was designed by Guy Carlander, architect of the Fisk Building and the El Coronado Lodge at Palo Duro Canyon.

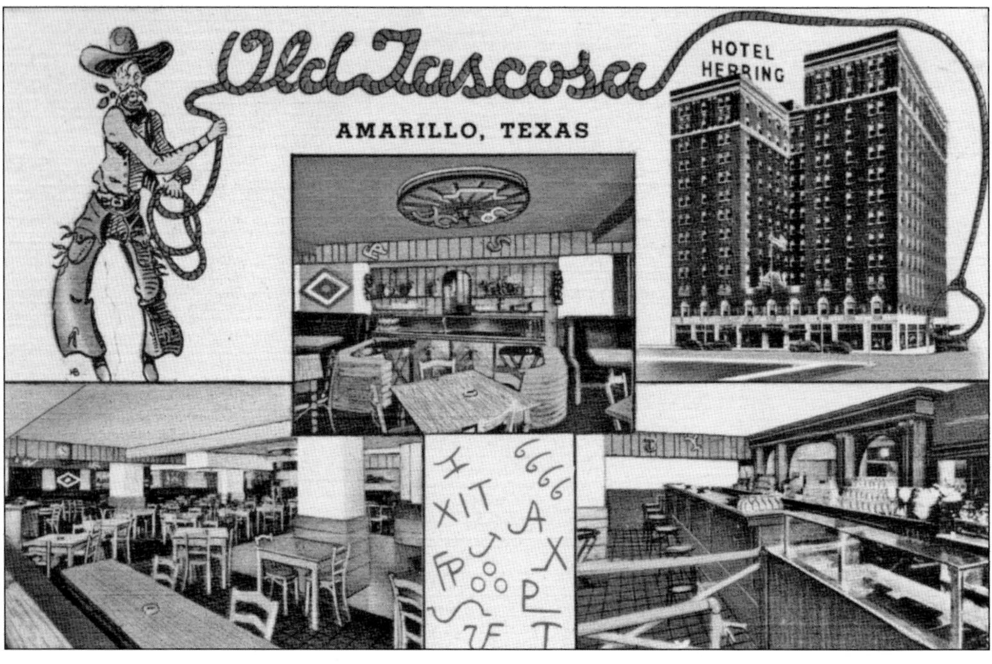

The Hotel Amarillo at Third Avenue and Polk Street was "The Panhandle's Meeting Place," the social and business center of Amarillo between 1889 and 1965. The old frame structure was replaced with a four-story brick building built by Gen. Ernest O. Thompson in 1922. The 12-story tower was added in 1927. The hotel was demolished with explosives on April 10, 1965.

Many celebrities stayed at the Capitol Hotel just off Route 66, which was an example of elegance during the oil boom. It originally had a lighted dome on the top designed to make it look like a capitol building. The Capitol Hotel featured lavish use of marble and beautiful murals. It closed in October 1971 and was torn down in 1977.

Polk Street was once called "America's best-lighted main street." This photograph looks north on Polk from Ninth Avenue towards Route 66 (Sixth Avenue). The Paramount Theater opened on April 21, 1932, and closed on March 20, 1975. It was converted to offices, but the sign was rescued from a nearby adult business and restored in 2006. The Fisk Building at left is now a hotel.

Owners Tillman and Mickey McCafferty are at left in this postcard view of the Aristocrat Café. It was in operation from 1945 to 1957 at 117 West Sixth Avenue and was named the best restaurant in Amarillo by the American Restaurant Association in 1948. The site is now a parking lot. Mickey went on to operate Mickey's Café on West Seventh Avenue for many years.

The Angelus Hotel at West Sixth Avenue and Van Buren Street had 66 rooms, so when Route 66 was routed down Sixth Avenue, the motel adopted the slogan "66 Rooms on Highway 66." The building also housed Angelus Drugs. The motel closed in 1961, and the building later housed a printing company before being demolished for a parking lot.

Terry Lomax introduced fine Mexican food to Amarillo in 1932. His Original Mexican Inn, at West Sixth Avenue and Van Buren Street, was known for live dance music. Ralph and Tim Pellow took over in 1945. Terry returned and it became Lomax's Fine Foods in 1954. Lomax operated several restaurants, including the well-known El Rancho. (Courtesy of Steve Rider.)

Cunningham Floral Company was founded in 1907 and moved to 2511 West Sixth Avenue in 1922. Founder Charles C. Cunningham died in 1924, and his wife, Carrie, ran the store until 1947. It was later operated by Juanita Blake. This postcard boasted that the building had 15,000 square feet of glass. It later became a nightclub and still stands today.

The Harley Davidson dealership, operated by the MCY company, opened in 1914. They also sold Cushman scooters and Schwinn bicycles. In September 1948, they were offering a Harley Davidson 125 for $350. By the 1950s, the dealership was known as the Harley Davidson Company and Beers Marine Supply. The building still stands.

Guests checking into the west wing of the Elk Courts, at 1401 West Sixth Avenue, pulled their cars into the garages and climbed stairs inside to their second-story rooms. Tom Shell, who worked for Texaco, constructed the complex in 1946. The Elk Courts became apartments, which have been demolished. (Courtesy of Steve Rider.)

The Cottage Camp at 1600 West Sixth Avenue was the only tourist court between Oklahoma City and Tucumcari when it opened in 1924. It started out with 13 cabins, but grew to cover the entire block with 49 units. Partly as a result of this facility's success, the city closed its municipal outdoor camp located a block off Route 66. (Courtesy of Devil's Rope Museum.)

Dock Henry Coffey's original Pontiac dealership was a small building on Tyler. He threw a huge two-day celebration when his new building occupying the entire 2100 block of West Sixth Avenue opened in June 1956. Coffey sold to Elmer Brown and E.E. Russell in 1964. The old dealership is now a U-Haul moving and storage facility.

Northwest Texas Hospital on West Sixth Avenue, the city's second hospital, opened on March 22, 1924. It was expanded in 1940, 1960, and 1968, eventually reaching a capacity of 275 beds. Northwest Texas Hospital moved to its current location in the Harrington Regional Medical Center in March 1982, and this complex became a retirement community.

The San Jacinto Heights Addition, west of downtown Amarillo, was first developed as a streetcar suburb along West Sixth Avenue between 1905 and 1915. The roadway was improved with gravel in 1921, the first improved route west from Amarillo. The neighborhood changed forever when the road was paved and designated US 66 in 1926. (Courtesy of Texas Department of Transportation.)

These members of the Sixth Street Committee were promoting Route 66 in 1939. West Sixth Avenue (popularly known as Sixth Street) between Georgia and Forest Streets is now a vibrant neighborhood of restaurants, nightclubs, and antique stores. It contains dozens of intact structures from the Route 66 era and is listed in the National Register of Historic Places. (Courtesy of *Route 66 Magazine* Collection.)

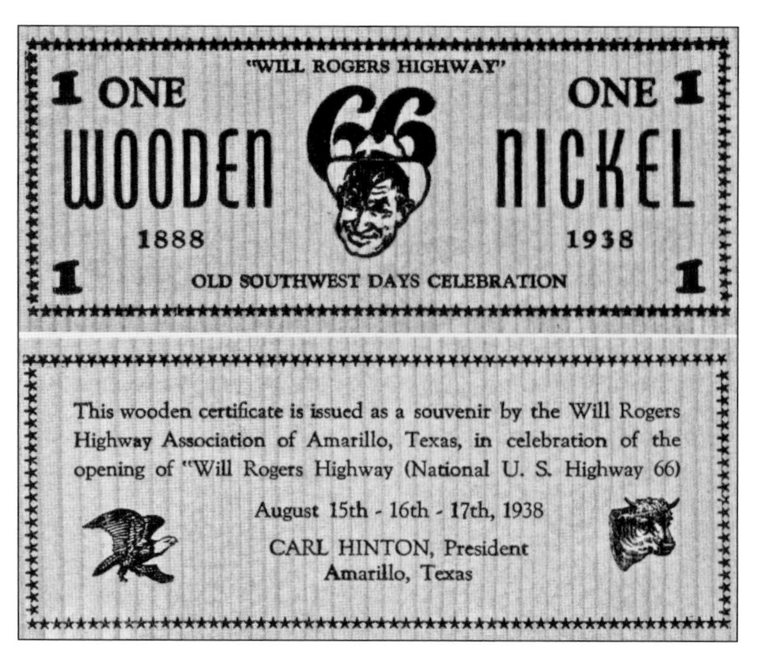

In August 1938, Amarillo hosted ceremonies dedicating Route 66 as the Will Rogers Highway. A big parade included Mrs. Will Rogers and Will's favorite horse, Soapsuds. Motorcades from Chicago and Los Angeles met in Amarillo and a pageant with a cast of 1,500 depicted 400 years of Southwest history. This wooden nickel was a souvenir of the event. (Courtesy of Steve Rider.)

The Natatorium or "Nat" is the best-known landmark on West Sixth Avenue. The open-air pool opened on July 15, 1922, and the structure was added in 1923. J.D. Tucker converted it into a ballroom in 1926, covering the pool with a maple hardwood floor. The Nat hosted performers such as Elvis Presley, Buddy Holly, and Duke Ellington before closing in the 1960s. Kasey Robinson has turned the restored landmark into an antique mall.

"Fist" Ansley only hired men as car hops for his Pig Hip Sandwich Shop, supposedly to keep women from being exposed to profanity. In 1934, he sold the Pig Hip and opened the Musical Pig Drive-In across the street. It closed in 1942. Ansley also served as president of the national Route 66 Association from 1936 to 1938 and ran Prairie Dog Town on Route 66 on the east side of Amarillo. (Courtesy of *Route 66 Magazine* Collection.)

The Golden Light Café at 2908 West Sixth Avenue is the oldest restaurant on Route 66 in Texas still operating at the same location. Chester "Pop" Ray and his wife Louise opened the café in 1946, and it has had four more owners since Pop retired in 1957. The Golden Light is named for the western sun that lights the café in the afternoon.

Mom Sherrod's Sagebrush Inn was located in the former Borden's Heap-O-Cream ice cream parlor, a building with Art Deco touches at 3120 West Sixth Avenue. Mom advertised "No beer, no wine, but a nice place to dine." The building was restored by Preservation Amarillo and a group of Boy Scouts in 1990, and it housed Pink Flamingo Antiques as of 2013.

Several historic gas stations in the historic district are serving new purposes today while retaining their historic integrity. This nightspot occupies the former Taylor's Texaco, a white porcelain–covered station at 3512 West Sixth Avenue. Constructed in 1937, Taylor's used the familiar standardized Texaco design by Walter D. Teague, featuring a canopy over the pump island.

Herbert Martin operated his Phillips 66 station at 3821 West Sixth Avenue from 1944 until 1991. The building was originally a Phillips cottage-style station, designed to blend in with the surrounding neighborhood. Herb was known for helping those who could not afford to pay for gas, and also occasionally allowed travelers to spend the night at the station. (Courtesy of Devil's Rope Museum.)

Herbert Martin's cottage-style station was replaced by the new Phillips 66 exaggerated modern design in 1963. The new stations were designed by Clarence Reinhardt, and included angled plate glass and bay entrances as well as a triangular canopy over the pump island. The building still stands today and houses an auto glass company. (Courtesy of Devil's Rope Museum.)

There was plenty of Western imagery at the Ranch-O-Tel, constructed in 1940 at 2501 West Sixth Avenue. It offered cowhide lampshades, horseshoe-shaped mirrors, and curtain rods resembling branding irons. Owners Chester and Betty Bordwell sold after mainline Route 66 was shifted to Amarillo Boulevard, and the Ranch-O-Tel became an apartment building, now listed in the National Register of Historic Places.

This postcard highlights the many opportunities for recreation in Amarillo. The back pointed out that Amarillo "has an invigorating 3676-foot altitude, 81% sunshine, cool nights in summer, moderate winters and year-round golf." The lower left panel shows pro golfer George Aulbach, the pro at the Amarillo Country Club. The country club opened on Route 66 in 1930.

In the fall of 1953, the new extension of Eighth Avenue (Amarillo Boulevard) west was completed, and the original Fillmore Street, Sixth Avenue, Bushland Boulevard, and Ninth Avenue alignment became Business Route 66. Both routes met "the Circle," shown here. This section was bypassed when Interstate 40 opened on November 15, 1968.

The Veteran's Administration Hospital was constructed by the Works Progress Administration in 1939 and dedicated on May 12, 1940. Cattle were raised on the 360-acre site, and gardens were maintained to feed the patients. Remodeled several times, it is now known as the Thomas E. Creek Department of Medical Affairs Medical Center.

The Sunset Motel was also located on the Circle. It was owned by George and Diamond Angeleos and then by Starvo and Lillie Higgins. This beautiful postcard advertised 20 modern units with famous Franciscan furnishings, private tile baths, air conditioning, and furnace heating. It became the Astro Motel at 5703 West Amarillo Boulevard.

The Broncho Lodge opened in 1952 on the traffic circle. The original sign featured a cowboy riding a bucking bronco, but it was modernized in the late 1950s. The restaurant, "Home of the Chuckwagon Spread," was operated by Oscar and Mamie Neal and later by Jim and Betty Jo Hedgecock. The Broncho Lodge later became the Friendship Inn Bronco Motel.

The Skyline Motel and Coffee Shop also opened in 1952 on the traffic circle. The address was originally 5711 West Ninth Avenue, now 6011 West Amarillo Boulevard. Ralph Cox was the original owner, and Elmer Dowell and his wife took over after a short time. They sold to Ray Lawson in 1977, and the motel is still standing in 2013 as an Economy Inn.

The Stardust Motel was located on the Circle where Business Route 66 met the bypass, across from Veteran's Hospital. The 21-unit motel offered air conditioning, free television, and a swimming pool. Leflar's Pancake House, operated by Eli and Maynette Leflar, was open around the clock. Eli was a former Amarillo police officer.

Advertised as the "finest in town," the Model Motel was located at 6640 West Amarillo Boulevard. Managed by Ben and Ann Watkins, it had 25 units and a restaurant on the premises. There was also a big wading pool and a children's playground. The restaurant building was still standing as of 2013, but most of the motel complex has been razed.

Ken Bourland operated the Amarillo Ranch 66 Motel, which had an appropriate address of 6666 West 66. Described by AAA in 1954 as "a first class court," it consisted of 31 units. The Ranch 66 and the Holiday Inn were the first two motels in Amarillo with a swimming pool. It later became the Guest House Motor Inn, and the complex now houses a restaurant and offices. (Courtesy of Steve Rider.)

Located two miles outside the city limits, the Arrow Court advertised "a clean, quiet place for a good night's rest." It was operated by Mr. and Mrs. R.A. Gilkerson, and later by Mr. and Mrs. O.E. Allen. The name had been changed to the Arrow Motel by the time of this photograph. The Tam O'Shanter Restaurant was located next door. The complex is now a private residence.

Amarillo became the helium capitol of the world with the discovery of the Cliffside gas field and the establishment of the US helium plant in 1929. Nearly all of the world's helium was processed here until 1943. It was phased out beginning in 1998. The abandoned facility is now surrounded by a fence topped with barbed wire. A sign reads: "All copper has been stolen from this facility. Keep Out."

West of Amarillo, a row of 10 vintage Cadillacs covered with graffiti is half buried in the ground at the same angle as the Pyramid of Cheops. The Cadillac Ranch was created by a trio of artists known as the Ant Farm Collective for the eccentric Stanley Marsh "3" (he insists his name is not Stanley Marsh "the third") and is shown here just after completion in 1974. Models from 1949 to 1963 stand as a symbol of a time when these tail-finned beauties ruled the road.

In 1997, Marsh decided urban sprawl was encroaching on the Cadillac Ranch. The Caddys were dug up and replanted two miles to the west. Marsh even ordered the litter from the old site gathered up and scattered around the new location. Ten holes remained at the old location, along with a sign that said "Unmarked graves for sale or rent." Although strongly identified with Route 66, the Cadillac Ranch was not located on 66 until it was moved.

Six

OLDHAM AND DEAF SMITH COUNTIES

Cal Farley's Boys Ranch is well off Route 66, but there is a connection. Cal Farley was a professional baseball player and wrestler who also once owned the Wun-Stop-Duzzit tire shop and a pair of gas stations on Route 66 in Amarillo. In 1939, he founded "America's First Boys Ranch" at the site of Old Tascosa, on land donated by Julian Bivins.

Outlaws such as Billy the Kid and legendary lawmen like Pat Garret and Bat Masterson walked the streets of Old Tascosa, the second town founded in the Panhandle. It was founded in 1876. These patrons of Ryan's Saloon are pictured after guns were banned in the town. Tascosa faded when the cattle drives ended, and the county seat moved to Vega in 1915. (Courtesy of Vega Public Library.)

Boot Hill Cemetery at Old Tascosa is the final resting place for 27 men who died in gunfights when the town was the raucous "Cowboy Capitol of the Panhandle." That includes four cowboys who "died with their boots on" in a single gunfight in 1886. Boys who spent a night alone in the cemetery became members of the Boys Ranch Boot Hill Club.

Two miles east of Bushland, Route 66 originally made a treacherous "S" curve through this narrow Rock Island Railroad underpass with a 14-foot clearance. A new four-lane highway bypassed the "Death Trap" overpass in 1951. William Henry Bush, owner of the Frying Pan Ranch, laid out a town he called "Bush Stop" in 1908. His wife decided Bushland was a better name. (Courtesy of Texas Department of Transportation.)

In 1928, a newspaper report described Wildorado as "the most plundered town in the United States," citing eight robberies at the Wildorado State Bank in the past three years. Nearly all the businesses were destroyed when Interstate 40 blasted through, leaving little more than a few grain elevators and the railroad depot, which was relocated a block away.

C. Orval Davis moved to Wildorado in 1929 and worked as a carpenter. He made concrete forms, many of which were used for culverts on Route 66. Davis served as postmaster and built the Davis Mercantile in 1947. It was a popular gathering place because Davis once owned the only television in town. The store was demolished for Interstate 40 in the 1960s. (Courtesy of Vega Public Library.)

The traveler may smell the most prominent feature of Wildorado well before they reach it and continue to smell it long after they have left. The horizon is filled with cattle at the massive Classic Cattle Feeders lot along Interstate 40 and Route 66. The Oldham County Chamber of Commerce says the feedlot handles about 20,000 head of cattle at a time.

Dub Edmonds and Jesse Fincher were operating Jesse's Café in Adrian when Interstate 40 opened, so they decided to open another Jesse's at Wildorado. The café was famous for Jesse's pies. They operated both restaurants until 1976 and then sold the Adrian location. Jesse died in 1989, and Dub Edmonds sold the Wildorado location in 1991.

This 1940s postcard shows some of the wildlife found along Route 66 in the Panhandle. The Nine-banded armadillo has come to symbolize the Texas roadside because so many end up as roadkill. An armadillo instinctively leaps straight up into the air when startled, right into the undercarriage of the vehicle. The word *armadillo* means "little armored one" in Spanish.

Vega was settled in 1899 and became the Oldham County seat in 1915. The name means "grassy meadow" in Spanish. The Ozark Trail Highway and original dirt Route 66 went through the square and past the courthouse before turning west. Route 66 was paved and relocated to the south in 1937. The original hipped roof of the courthouse was removed in 1967.

Looking west on Route 66 in Vega, Hill's Café is at left. It became the Prairie Hills Café under the ownership of Loudine and Harvey Floyd in 1961, and a much larger sign (with "café" spelled out inside four diamond shapes) was erected. The sign still stands at the Hickory Inn east of the former café building. Orville Henry Groneman operated the Gulf station at right.

The Bonanza Motel in Vega is still in business today. It was operated by Mr. and Mrs. E.C. Dodgin when this photograph was taken and was billed as "three blocks east of the red light" in Vega. Ads for the 24-unit motel also mention a children's playground and a restaurant next door. It was also operated at one time by Ezra J. and Grace Windom.

In 1924, "Colonel" J.T. Owen opened his Magnolia station on the dirt Ozark Trail in Vega. Edward and Cora Wilson later leased it and lived upstairs. Their son Austin took over in 1933. The Slatz Barbershop occupied the building from 1953 to 1965. The station has been restored by the community of Vega and the Oldham County Chamber of Commerce.

Roark Hardware is the oldest hardware store still operating on Route 66 and traces its roots to Western Hardware and Lumber, shown here. Western became Lone Star Hardware, operated by cousins R.C. "Lysle" Godwin and Claude Morris. They constructed the present building in 1929. Claude's daughter Shirley married Bud Roark, and their son Randy manages the business today.

The Vega Motel is one of the best-preserved motels on Route 66 in Texas. It opened in the early 1940s as the Vega Court, and was operated by E.M and Josephine Pancoast. They sold to Ethridge Betts in the early 1970s, and Harold and Tresa Whaley took over in 1981. Vince Gill shot the video for his song "I Never Knew Lonely" in room 21.

The Sands Motel on the western outskirts of Vega was constructed for Jimmie and Mamie McCasland, who once operated restaurants on Route 66 in Groom. It opened October 25, 1963, with "42 ultra modern units" and the "Finest free television in the West" It is now the Best Western Country Inn.

Dot Leavitt operated Zero Lockers in Vega, a refrigerated storage facility that once sold the only ice on 66 between Amarillo and Tucumcari. She spent decades gathering antiques and Western artifacts for Dot's Mini Museum, opened in 1963. Dot passed away in December 2000 and her daughter Betty now manages the museum on the original 1926 Route 66 alignment.

Landergrin was once the bustling headquarters of the LS Ranch. In 1996, this isolated spot hosted the "Run to the Heartland," the first of the modern, national Route 66 conventions. At that time, George Rook and his wife, Melba, were operating Route 66 Antiques and the Neon Soda Saloon here. George displayed the largest known collection of Route 66 signs inside, but the signs were sold and the business was abandoned after he died in 1998.

Former Texas Ranger Calvin Grant Aten shot it out with rustlers on Christmas Day 1889 before becoming the first settler in the Adrian area. Adrian was officially founded and named after farmer Adrian Cullen in 1909, when the Chicago, Rock Island & Gulf Railway came through. The Giles Hotel, later the Adrian Mercantile and Community Center, still stands.

Adrian is proud of its status as the "Geo-mathematical Center of Route 66." A sign across from the Midpoint Café declares a distance off 1,139 miles to Chicago and 1,139 miles to Los Angeles and serves as a popular photo op stop. The late Route 66 author and historian Tom Snyder first declared that Adrian was the mathematical midway point.

Zella Crim was a waitress who dreamed of owning her own café. In 1928, she leased a simple building with a dirt floor in Adrian and opened it as Zella's Café. Dub Edmonds and former Navy cook Jesse Fincher expanded the building in 1956 and made it Jesse's Cafe. They added an A-frame apartment on top in 1965. The café was so popular that Dub and Jesse opened another location in Wildorado when Interstate 40 bypassed Adrian.

Jesse's became Peggy's Café, owned by Peggy Crietz, and later by Bob and Ann Wood. Rachel Ruiz then renamed it Rachel's, and it was later owned by Ronnie Johnson. The living quarters above the café were removed after a fire. It became the Adrian Café when Fran Houser took over in 1991. By 1995, she was calling it the Midpoint. The Midpoint, now owned by Dennis Purschwitz, was the inspiration for Flo's V-8 Café in Pixar's animated film *Cars*.

In 1947, the café and station at the Kozy Kottage Kamp burned down. Bob Harris, a former employee of the camp, brought a war surplus control tower to the site for his new café. It was nicknamed the "Bent Door" because the door was bent to match the sloped windows of the tower. It later became Tommy's, operated by the Loveless family. Tommy's closed in 1970, but Roy and Ramona Kiewert are working to restore the landmark.

Percy Gruhlkey established a service station in the front section of his home about five miles west of Adrian in the 1930s. In 1946, he erected the cinder block structure shown here to house his Cap Rock Service Station. There was no electricity for many years, so wind generators charged the batteries for the pumps. Interstate 40 killed the business, but the structure still stands. (Courtesy of Russell Olsen.)

This group posed at the state line during the glory days of Glenrio, when the highway bustled with traffic. Route 66 was widened here in 1955 but the four-lane highway ended at Glenrio for many years. Drivers braved an overloaded two lane highway west to Tucumcari that was dubbed "Slaughter Lane" in the late 1960s.

This Tourist Information Bureau station, shown in 1940, greeted Route 66 travelers as they entered Texas at Glenrio. The center offered maps and assistance, including water for overheated radiators, and was demolished in 1955. Glenrio once had many businesses serving travelers. Scenes for the 1940 Dust Bowl epic *The Grapes of Wrath* were filmed here.

Gas stations at Glenrio were in Texas because the taxes were lower. Deaf Smith County, Texas, was dry, so the bars were on the New Mexico side. Homer and Margaret Ehresman ran the State Line Bar from 1934 to 1946, when they left amid rumors of a bypass. Learning that construction was still years away, they returned to open the Texas Longhorn Motel in 1950.

Glenrio died when Interstate 40 opened in September 1973. Only ruins and tumbleweeds greet the occasional visitor today. The shattered sign at the Texas Longhorn Motel and Café once declared it was the "Last Stop in Texas" on the east side and "First Stop in Texas" on the west. A new Texas Longhorn was built on the interstate near Endee, New Mexico, but was abandoned in the 1980s.

The diner operated by the Joseph Brownlee family beginning in 1952 was designed to resemble the sleek pre-fabricated Valentine Diners made in Wichita, Kansas. It is actually made of cinder blocks and concrete and was later known as the Little Juarez Diner. The fictional town of Radiator Springs in the animated movie *Cars* includes an abandoned building just like the Little Juarez that becomes a racing museum.

Route 66 was officially decertified in 1985. On October 31, 1986, Texas Department of Highways and Public Safety employee Elmer Olle was preparing 277 Route 66 signs from across the Panhandle for auction. The media reported that the signs were expected to bring from $40 to $80 at the auction in Austin on November 21–22. (Courtesy of Steve Rider.)